GIBRALTAR

GIBRALTAR

Claude Doak

CHELSEA HOUSE

LV4-005086

Library of Congress Cataloging-in-Publication Data

Doak, Claude.
  Gibraltar.
  Includes index.
  Summary: An introduction to the history, topography, economy,
politics, industry, people, and culture of this British dependency on
the southern coast of Spain.

  1. Gibraltar. [1. Gibraltar]
  I. Title.   II. Series.
  DP302.G36D63   1986   946'.89   86-11690

  ISBN 1-55546-155-7

Editorial Director: Susan R. Williams
Senior Editor: Rebecca Stefoff
Associate Editor: Rafaela Ellis
Art Director: Maureen McCafferty
Series Designer: Anita Noble
Project Coordinator: Kathleen P. Luczak

ACKNOWLEDGEMENTS

The author and publishers are grateful to the following organizations for information
and photographs: Gibraltar Tourist Office; National Air and Space Administration; Wide
World Photos, Inc. Picture research: Imagefinders, Inc.

Contents

NORWAY

SWEDEN

DENMARK

U.S.S.R.

UNITED KINGDOM

BELGIUM
NETHERLANDS

GERMAN DEM. REP.

POLAND

LUXEMBOURG

CZECHOSLOVAKIA

FRANCE

FED. REP. OF GERMANY

SWITZERLAND

AUSTRIA

HUNGARY

ROMANIA

ITALY

YUGOSLAVIA

BULGARIA

CORSICA

Barcelona

MINORCA

ALBANIA

MAJORCA

SARDINIA

GREECE

TURKEY

M E D I T E R R A N E A N   S E A

Algiers

SICILY

TUNISIA

ALGERIA

LIBYA

Map: Carol Molyneaux

The Rock—
Key to the Mediterranean

On a narrow peninsula of Spain's southern Mediterranean coast, at the tip of the Spanish province of Andalusia, lies Gibraltar, the British colony famous for the Rock of Gibraltar—perhaps the most well-known symbol in the world for strength and security. "As solid as the Rock of Gibraltar" is a phrase heard around the world.

Surrounded by the sea, Gibraltar has been a strategic fortress for centuries

8

Yet while the Rock of Gibraltar is large, the colony of Gibraltar is very small. Nevertheless, it is one of the most important strategic places on earth. Whoever occupies Gibraltar controls all sea traffic into and out of the Mediterranean Sea. This strategic importance has determined the history of Gibraltar and its people.

The name "Gibraltar" is a corruption of the Arabic *Jabal Tariq* or "Tariq's mountain," a name given to the mountain by the troups of Tariq Ibn Ziyad, a leader of the Muslim Moorish army that invaded and conquered the peninsula in 711 A.D. Over the centuries, Jabal Tariq has come to be pronounced Gibraltar. Gibraltarians refer to it as "The Rock," and the Spanish call it *El Peñón*, which means "The Big Rock."

Rising 1,396 feet (426 meters) above sea level, the Rock of Gibraltar dominates the entire peninsula and all the area around it. Ever since the invention of gunpowder and the use of cannons in warfare, the Rock of Gibraltar has been the key to controlling the Strait of Gibraltar, the narrow waterway that connects the Mediterranean and the Atlantic Ocean. The history of the Rock of Gibraltar is a history of struggle to control this important strategic piece of land.

Control of the Rock was once important for economic as well as military reasons. As ships ventured beyond the confines of the Mediterranean to seek new trade routes to other parts of the world, control of the Rock of Gibraltar meant control of com-

Tariq Tower was built in the 8th century by the Moorish army

A fortress wall bears the scars of 18th-century cannon fire

merce in the Mediterranean. Also, because of its strategic location between Europe and Africa, Gibraltar itself was an important trading place where merchants from both continents could trade goods. Muslim merchants from Africa could bring their spices, cloth, and finely wrought jewelry to trade with merchants from Italy, Spain, and France who offered gold, metal products, and other finished goods. Gibraltar was and continues to be a cosmopolitan city, with people from all over the world meeting in this tiny colony.

Today Gibraltar is an important military base for England and the North Atlantic Treaty Organization (NATO), of which the

11

United States is a member. The headquarters for two of NATO's commands are located on the peninsula. While some people may believe that in the age of atomic bombs Gibraltar has lost its strategic importance, most military experts believe that possession of the Rock is just as important as it ever was. For NATO and the British, Gibraltar provides an important naval base with large areas for repairing and resupplying ships. Britain also has an airport on the peninsula; it serves both military and commercial airplanes.

Recently, the Spanish government has demanded that Gibraltar be returned to Spanish control. These demands have led to some friction between the Spanish and British governments, but representatives from both sides have held a series of meetings that have led to some progress in settling the issue. For the present, Gibraltar continues to be an important British military base with a large military garrison and a cosmopolitan civilian population that enjoys a mild climate, a unique lifestyle, and a growing tourist trade.

Geography and Climate

Geologists believe that tens of thousands of years ago the Rock of Gibraltar and the peninsula on which it is located were part of a land bridge that joined Europe and Africa. These scientists—who study the physical nature and history of the earth—say that the matching limestone rock and fossils found on Gibraltar and on the opposite Moroccan coast prove that a bridge of land joining the two continents once existed.

In 1848, the skull of a Neanderthal man was discovered in a cave on the Rock. This was the first Neanderthal skull ever found. Its finders did not realize its importance, however, and it was not until years later that the significance of the discovery became clear. The cave has since been covered by a large rockslide, so searchers can no longer get into the cave to see what other discoveries might be made. The skull, which is known as the Gibraltar Man, is now the prized possession of the Royal College of Surgeons in London, England.

Anthropologists—who study the origins, physical and cultural characteristics, distribution, and variety of human beings—believe that Neanderthals were a widespread subspecies of prehistoric humans who lived in parts of Europe, Africa, and Asia from

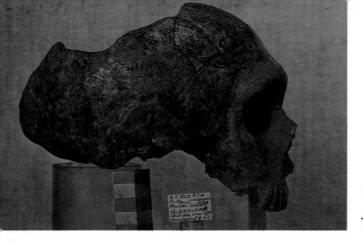

A profile of the skull of Gibraltar Man, the first Neanderthal skull discovered

about 125,000 to about 40,000 years ago. Neanderthals were the immediate predecessors of today's people. They were shorter and had a thicker physical build than modern humans, and they had longer skulls, with lower foreheads and heavier eyebrow ridges. Their upright posture and brain size, however, resembled those of modern humans. Moreover, anthropologists say that Neanderthals made sophisticated stone tools, which indicates a high intelligence.

The name "Neanderthal" comes from the Neander Valley, which is near Düsseldorf, Germany. In 1848, the same year that the Neanderthal skull was discovered in Gibraltar, men working in a quarry in the Neander Valley accidentally discovered what was later declared to be the first Neanderthal skeleton remains. Since Germany is so far from Gibraltar, some scientists have suggested that when Gibraltar was part of the land bridge that connected the two continents, Neanderthals traveled over the bridge from Africa to Europe. Some of the Neanderthals probably lived in the many caves in the Rock, as they afford ready-made protection.

Gibraltar was, therefore, important to the development of the human race. The caves of Gibraltar have been the source of a wide variety of fossils and other evidence that the rock has been used by humans through the ages. Just as Gibraltar is important today, so it was important tens of thousands of years ago.

Geologists also believe that much of the Rock of Gibraltar was at one time below water. Now it rises majestically above the narrow peninsula on which it is located, overlooking the peninsula and the strait. The peninsula seems just big enough for the Rock and nothing else, yet people have found room for a small city, a large naval base, and an airport.

The Gibraltar peninsula is just 3 miles (5 kilometers) long and three-fourths of a mile (1.2 kilometers) wide. It covers 2.25 square

The view from high atop the Rock includes the Bay of Gibraltar

miles (5.8 square kilometers), making it just slightly larger than the entire area of Central Park in New York City. The peninsula is connected to the Spanish mainland by a mile-long (1.6 kilometers) narrow, sandy isthmus only 10 feet (3 meters) above sea level.

The low, flat isthmus ends suddenly with the dramatic rise of the imposing Rock. The Rock is 1,380 feet tall (412 meters) at this northernmost point. From here it forms a jagged ridge, which rises quickly to the maximum height of 1,396 feet (425 meters), 150 feet (46 meters) higher than the Empire State Building. It then runs south for almost 2 miles (3 kilometers) until it suddenly drops off in a series of shelves down to the sea at Europa Point, the southernmost point of the peninsula, which faces Morocco.

The Rock of Gibraltar itself is composed of gray limestone, overlaid in places with dark shale. From the Mediterranean or eastern side, it appears to be a series of sheer, almost vertical and inaccessible cliffs that drop to the huge sand slopes rising above Catalan Bay and Sandy Bay. On the Atlantic or western side, the slope rises more gradually. On this side, many houses have been built for the people who live on the Rock.

The southern end of the Rock towers above two wide platforms that look something like plains but are composed of solid rock. The platforms are located one above the other and were flattened or cut out by waves long ago when the sea level was much higher than it is now. The higher platform, which is approximately 300 to 400 feet (90 to 125 meters) above sea level, is called Windmill Hill Flats. It runs southward until it ends in a sharp cliff 200 feet (60 meters) high. The second and lower of the two plat-

The Rock looms large over the Spanish Bay in a 19th-century photo

forms is called Europa Flats. This platform ends at the Mediterranean with cliffs 50 to 100 feet (15 to 30 meters) high. Thus on two of its four sides—the eastern and the southern—the Rock of Gibraltar presents sheer, inaccessible cliffs.

On the western side, where the slope of the Rock is much less severe, there is a large natural harbor; over the years it has been enlarged and improved by the addition of artificial breakwaters. Gibraltar Harbor covers about 440 acres (180 hectares) and is divided into commercial and military ports. The northern part of

Yachts are moored at the new marina in Gibraltar Harbor

the harbor serves the colony's commercial and private shipping traffic, while the southern part of the harbor serves as a British and NATO naval base. The Royal Gibraltar Yacht Club located in this harbor is one of the oldest such clubs outside England.

Just north of the harbor, jutting into Gibraltar Bay (or "Algeciras Bay," as the Spanish call it) on the western side of the peninsula, is the Gibraltar airport. Its runway, built of stone blasted from the Rock, cuts across the entire northern part of the isthmus just below the border with Spain. Half of the runway's 1,800-foot (549 meters) length extends into Gibraltar Bay. Commercial aircraft share the runway with aircraft from the British Royal Air Force and military airplanes from NATO countries. Because the only road to Spain crosses the runway, drivers must wait for a green light between landings and takeoffs before they can leave Gibraltar.

The Rock of Gibraltar is anything but solid. There are 78 known natural caverns in the Rock, the largest of which is a magnificent Gothic-like chamber over 70 feet (21 meters) high, with an entrance 1,000 feet (305 meters) above sea level. It is used today as a concert hall. In addition to these caves, there are almost

The road to Spain crosses the runway of Gibraltar's airport

The Rock is riddled with caverns; in St. Michael's Cave, stalactites and stalagmites form a natural cathedral

A British soldier guards Gibraltar's summit in this 19th-century illustration

35 miles (56 kilometers) of man-made tunnels—as compared to only 25 miles (40 kilometers) of open highway on the entire peninsula.

Other large galleries have been carved out of the Rock. During World War II, the British army's engineering corps, the Royal Engineers, built an entire city—hospitals, barracks, dumps, work-

20

shops, and command posts—deep within the Rock.

All of these natural and man-made passages, galleries, reservoirs, and caverns make the Rock of Gibraltar resemble a giant piece of Swiss cheese. But there is no danger that they have weakened it in any way. So large is the Rock that all of these tunnels and caves amount to only a small portion of its total area.

Tourists and Gibraltarians alike can enjoy a walk through Alameda Gardens

What soil exists on the peninsula has been formed from weather-worn limestone. Around the city of Gibraltar and to the south there is red sand, while more than half of the eastern slopes are covered by beige sand. Geologists believe that the sand on the eastern slopes was blown there from the Sahara desert across the Strait of Gibraltar.

More than 500 species of small flowering plants are found on Gibraltar. The Gibraltar candytuft is a flower found only on the Rock, and many different kinds of wild plants grow on the Rock's upper slopes. Fig, olive, orange, and pine trees, as well as hibiscus and bougainvillea plants, give Gibraltar a tropical appearance.

Gibraltar has wild rabbits and foxes, but the most famous animal is the Barbary ape, the only wild monkey in Europe. Gibraltar is also a sanctuary for many species of migratory birds and is the only breeding place and residence for the Barbary partridge. As hunting for sport is strictly limited by law, the birds on the peninsula are protected.

Gibraltar enjoys a mild Mediterranean climate. The average annual rainfall is 34 inches (865 millimeters), which comes mainly in the form of a few heavy showers. From June through mid-

September almost no rain falls. Temperatures during the year range from 55 to 85 degrees Fahrenheit (13 to 29 degrees Centigrade). Summer temperatures average about 71 degrees Fahrenheit (22 degrees Centigrade) and seldom rise much higher than 90 degrees Fahrenheit (33 degrees Centigrade).

The Levanter, a strong wind that blows from east to west in the Mediterranean, adds oppressive humidity to the summer temperatures. During the summer and into the fall, the prevailing Levanter—which blows against the eastern side of the Rock and swirls over its crest—is very damp and forms large, moisture-laden clouds. The top of the Rock is covered with dark clouds and the town of Gibraltar and the bay below are bathed in thick, sticky humidity. Were it not for the Levanter, the climate on Gibraltar, especially in the summer, would be perfect. Winters on Gibraltar are exceptionally mild, particularly for Europe.

Lush foliage flourishes in Gibraltar's Mediterranean climate

At the turn of the century, Caleta on Catalan Bay was a quaint village; today, it is being developed as a tourist area

The City of Gibraltar

The city of Gibraltar is located on the western side of the penin-sula next to Gibraltar Harbor. Except for the small fishing village of Caleta on Catalan Bay, which is being modernized as a tourist resort area, and Sandy Bay, also being developed exclusively for tourists, the city of Gibraltar is the only city on the peninsula.

Gibraltar has a total population of approximately 35,000: 30,000 civilians and 5,000 British military personnel and their families. For reasons of military security, the development of housing is strictly controlled. Civilians can live only in certain des-ignated areas. Added to this is the severe shortage of land suitable for building. Housing for the civilian population, therefore, is a serious problem, and while everyone lives comfortably in government-owned apartments, few Gibraltarians own houses.

Civilians live mainly in the northern end of the city of Gibral-tar, in houses and apartments built in tiers that stretch some 300 feet (91 meters) from the remains of the old defensive walls up the gradual slope of the western side. Government residences, mili-tary housing, and some new civilian housing are located south of the harbor on two level stretches of land and on the lower slopes of the Rock.

A sign bearing the Gibraltar flag—a Union Jack—welcomes visitors to the city

The drum major of the regiment symbolizes Gibraltar's devotion to British pomp

The city of Gibraltar today reflects the influence of all the different nations who conquered and lived on Gibraltar. A massive square tower remains from the large fortress the Moors once built. Other surviving Moorish structures include a bath and water cisterns. Along with the Moorish influences are those of the Spanish and British. All of these influences come together to make Gibraltar a fascinating mixture of old and new, Muslim and Christian.

The business and social center of the tiny city is Main Street, where tourists and sailors from around the world shop. They find a wealth of goods on display in shop windows, as well as a wide variety of food and entertainment. Policemen dressed in the uniforms of London's famous bobbies direct traffic under palm trees.

The tiered housing of modern Gibraltar sits in the shadow of an 8th-century Moorish mosque

The residential area in Gibraltar is one of the most spectacular in the world. Because there is not an inch of space to spare on the peninsula, houses cling to every possible ledge and crevice on the northwestern side of the Rock. Some of them look as if they might fall at any moment. Among the houses are hanging gardens, shaded lanes, and flowering creepers. The scent of mimosa fills the air, and orange and palm trees sprout up among the houses.

Spain is close to downtown Gibraltar

The Rock's summit can be reached by cable car

Scores of automobiles clog the narrow streets of the city

All the living areas on the peninsula are connected by an excellent road system. There are more than 6,000 automobiles on Gibraltar—about one car for every ten yards of pavement. Monumental traffic jams at rush hour are common. In addition to the airport, which provides regular flights to London and to Tangier, in Morocco, a car ferry crosses the strait daily to Tangier, and passenger liners stop every day at the port. Finally, a cable car ascends to the central summit of the Rock.

29

A History of Sieges

Evidence shows that Gibraltar has been occupied by humans since the Stone Age. Archaeologists have also found the fossilized bones and teeth of ancient bears, leopards, seals, and even elephants and rhinoceroses. Although the ancient Greeks knew about the Rock, it was the Phoenicians who settled on the peninsula more than 1,100 years B.C. Later, the Carthagenians (a warlike North African civilization) took control of the peninsula, only to be followed by the Romans, who controlled the Rock for more than 600 years and called it *Mons Calpe*.

On April 30, 711 A.D., a Muslim Moorish army commanded by the Berber leader Tariq Ibn Ziyad invaded and conquered Gibraltar and then went on to conquer Spain, which was at that time ruled by a Germanic people called the Visigoths (they had

A model of Tariq Ibn Ziyad stands in the Moorish Castle

30

The Moorish "Tower of Homage" remains intact after 12 centuries

invaded and conquered the Romans in Spain in the late 4th century A.D.). This invasion was the beginning of the 800-year Moorish domination of Spain and Gibraltar. In 725, the Moors built a massive fortress on Gibraltar, part of which remains today. Gibraltar was a military outpost only until 1160, when the Moorish conquerors founded a city. The Spanish regained control of the peninsula in 1309, but lost it to the Moors again in 1333. The Moors then heavily refortified the Rock and the peninsula.

After 150 years of intermittent but fierce warfare, during which Gibraltar changed hands eight times, the Spanish reconquered the peninsula in 1462. The Spanish forces were led by Don Alonso de Arcos, who took the fortress from the Moors forever. But Arcos left no mark on Gibraltar. He is buried in Seville, Spain, and the epitaph on his tomb says: "Here lies buried the honored knight don Alonso de Arcos, governor of Tarifa, who wrested Gibraltar from the enemies of our Holy Faith."

The fortress was turned over to the Duke of Medina Sidonia. For 16 years the Duke worked to improve the fortifications; he worked so diligently, in fact, that the King of Spain gave Gibraltar to the Duke and his heirs. The Duke gained the additional title Marques de Gibraltar (a marques is just below a duke).

When the Duke died in 1489, his son was required by law to ask Queen Isabella to confirm his titles and lands. When he did so, she declined to recognize his right to Gibraltar. Instead, she offered the young duke many other titles and lands if only he would turn over Gibraltar to her. The duke refused, and for 13 years the argument continued. Finally, in 1502, the two parties arrived at a settlement of their dispute and Gibraltar came under the direct control of the Spanish Crown. The Queen then granted a coat of arms to Gibraltar: a red castle with a golden key.

On Sunday, August 4, 1704, during the War of the Spanish Succession, a combined fleet of British and Dutch ships commanded by Sir George Rooke attacked Gibraltar. The fleet was originally supposed to attack Barcelona, Spain, but missed its opportunity to do so. The decision to invade and conquer Gibraltar was made at the last minute as an alternate plan.

Rooke had a fleet of 71 warships with 4,000 cannons, 26,000 artillerymen, and 9,000 soldiers. When the commander of the fortress at Gibraltar, General Diego Salinas, refused to surrender, Rooke attacked.

Salinas had only 80 trained soldiers and 20 working cannons. When Rooke lined up his fleet just 500 yards (365 meters) from the western side of the fort and opened fire, the battle was as good as over. Within five hours the fleet had fired more than 15,000 cannon balls into the city and fortress. After this furious bombardment, the British invaded and quickly captured Gibraltar.

After taking possession, the British sacked the city but allowed the Spanish residents to choose whether they wanted to remain in Gibraltar or move to Spain. Fewer than 100 of the city's 6,000 residents chose to remain. The rest resettled across the isthmus in San Roque, where their descendants live today. To this day the Spanish government officially regards the residents of San Roque as citizens of Gibraltar.

In 1713, Britain and Spain signed the Treaty of Utrecht, which ended the hostilities and recognized the British capture of Gibraltar. The treaty, however, is still the source of much argument. The Spanish government claims that it allowed Britain only to maintain a military post on Gibraltar and does not give Britain possession of the peninsula. Britain, on the other hand, maintains that the treaty gave possession of Gibraltar to them and that the Spanish have no claim to the peninsula. You will read later in this book how disagreement over the meaning of this treaty continues even today, nearly 300 years later.

The Spanish made several attempts to recapture Gibraltar from the British. In 1726 Spain attacked Gibraltar with an army of 20,000 men. In four days they fired 14,000 cannon balls at Gibraltar. So furious was the barrage that the cannons of the attackers

melted. However, the fortifications on the peninsula were so strong that, despite the number of cannon balls shot at the British, only 26 men were killed.

Throughout its history, Gibraltar has faced 15 separate sieges, but the most famous was the siege of 1779 to 1783. This siege made the Rock the symbol of permanence and invulnerability it is today.

On July 11, 1779, during the American Revolution (when Britain was at war with France and Spain as well as the new American

Spain has fought for control of Gibraltar since it battled the Moors in 1309; today, Great Britain rules the Rock

Cannons defended the Rock during battles

nation), an army of 40,000 Spanish and French besiegers attacked Gibraltar across the peninsula. For three years and seven months a British garrison of fewer than 6,000 men, commanded by Lieutenant General George Augustus Eliot, held Gibraltar against what

seemed impossible odds. During the siege, opposing artillery batteries fired almost half a million shells at each other. During one six-week period in 1781, the attackers fired 76,000 shells into the fortifications on Gibraltar. Although this intense bombardment

The Spanish Armada assembled in the waters off Gibraltar before attacking England

A museum tableau depicts soldiers tunneling into the Rock

destroyed hundreds of houses on Gibraltar, only 70 men of the defending forces were killed.

A famous incident that occurred during the siege is recounted to this day. General Eliot became alarmed one day when he saw that the enemy lines were getting so close to the Rock that his gunners would not be able to lower their cannons enough to fire on the attackers. A cannon could fire on the attackers from only one place—an inaccessible ledge on the northeast face of the Rock. When General Eliot asked aloud how he could possibly place a cannon at that strategic but impossible spot, Sergeant

Major Ince of the Corps of Royal Artificers pointed out that the only way to reach the crucial ledge was by tunneling. At that moment the British army's engineering corps, the Royal Engineers, was born. It was also the birth of the huge tunnel network that now honeycombs the Rock.

The siege reached a climax on September 13, 1782, when the Spanish and French attacked by sea, using ten vessels that the French designed specifically for bombarding Gibraltar. Each of the vessels had up to 20 heavy brass cannons. The floating artillery batteries lined up half a mile off the west side of the Rock and opened fire. The British answered the barrage with 96 guns of their own. The British also had a new weapon—red-hot cannon balls that set fire to any ship they struck. In an artillery battle that lasted from early morning into the evening, both sides hurled countless shells at each other. As night settled on the battle, the attacking vessels burst into flames one by one.

General George Augustus Eliot secured Gibraltar for Britain

*This engraving illus-
trates the siege of
Gibraltar by France
and Spain in 1782*

Nelson (right) with army leader Welling-ton in the late 1700s

A plaque at Trafalgar Cemetery honors Nelson's men

TRAFALGAR CEMETERY
HERE LIE THE REMAINS OF SOME WHO
DIED OF WOUNDS AT GIBRALTAR AFTER
NELSON'S GREAT VICTORY IN OCTOBER,
1805, THOSE KILLED DURING THE BATTLE
HAVING BEEN BURIED AT SEA. OTHER
GRAVES DATE FROM 1798.

In October of 1782, the British navy relieved the troops on the Rock. Eliot and the British had broken the siege and Gibraltar was saved. Eliot became known as the "Cock of the Rock," the Hero of Gibraltar, and Gibraltar became a symbol of British power and endurance. With the Treaty of Versailles in 1783, Spain gave Gibraltar to Britain in exchange for the island of Minorca and confirmation of the Spanish title to Florida.

A plaque on the northern wall of Gibraltar bears this inscription:

> These walls suffered, on the 12th July, 1781, a Spanish bombardment estimated at about 150,000 balls and 60,000 thirteen-inch shells. One hundred and twenty of the defenders were killed and property in the town sustained eighty thousand pounds worth of damage. The fortifications were almost undamaged.

Gibraltarians also remember Lord Horatio Nelson, England's greatest naval commander. He is a hero in Gibraltar (as he is in Great Britain). In 1805, he led British ships to victory against a combined force of French and Spanish men-of-war in the Battle of Trafalgar, just west of Gibraltar. Although Nelson died from wounds received in the battle, his triumph over the enemy preserved Gibraltar for Great Britain and kept Britain itself safe from a French invasion.

Building a Prosperous Community

After the war with France and Spain ended, Britain concentrated on rebuilding and expanding Gibraltar. To encourage trade and attract settlers, the Rock was declared a free port. In 1830, it became a Crown Colony. Life on Gibraltar was not pleasant in those early days. A yellow fever epidemic carried off more than half of the tiny settlement's population, and those who remained faced privation, malnutrition, scurvy, profiteering, and political corruption. Because the colony was considered a military post, even civilians were subject to martial law. Drunkenness was a military crime, and public floggings and hangings took place.

Yet through all these hardships and difficulties, the population of Gibraltar not only grew but slowly began to build the prosperous colony the world knows today. When the Suez Canal opened in 1869, Gibraltar became an important military and supply post on the Mediterranean route from England to India.

Sephardic Jews, whose ancestors had been driven out of Spain during the Inquisition in 1492, came to Gibraltar from their exile in Morocco. Genoese traders, Portuguese sailors, Hindu merchants, discharged British soldiers, Spaniards, refugees from the French Revolution, and others found a home in the colony.

*By the late 19th century, Gibraltar's population was growing and its
steep hillsides were being covered with rows of houses*

*British troops kept Gibraltar
peaceful in the early 1900s*

Immigrants arriving from Morocco in the early 1900s

With the end of the seemingly constant sieges, the newcomers helped rebuild the shattered colony.

Across the isthmus, just out of range of the cannons of the day, grew the Spanish town of La Linea (The Lines), upon the site of the Spanish lines constructed during the great siege of 1779–1783. Today La Linea depends on Gibraltar for its economic prosperity, and people in La Linea and Gibraltar have close ties with each other.

During World War I Gibraltar was never directly threatened by military action. No bombs or shells fell on the peninsula during this war, as they had in wars past. But Gibraltar was an important military base, especially for the British navy. New dockyard facilities were built, and the large harbor, where convoys assembled and ships were repaired, was incessantly busy.

During the Great Depression of 1929–1938, a time of extreme economic hardship for most of the world, Gibraltar suffered less from the weakened world economy than many other places. Most of the colony's economy depended on the ships of the Royal Navy, so the dockyards and port facilities continued to operate and provide employment for a large number of Gibraltarians.

The Spanish Civil War broke out in 1936. Gibraltar was caught between opposing forces who battled on the nearby Spanish mainland and in neighboring waters. Although Gibraltar remained apart from the conflict, a flood of Spanish refugees came to the Rock to escape from the fighting. As the fighting moved north and away from the colony, however, life in Gibraltar returned to normal.

Unlike World War I, World War II was a traumatic experience for most Gibraltarians and brought hardship to the colony, including bombings from enemy airplanes. In 1942, as the danger of a possible German invasion receded, Gibraltar became the headquarters for the Allied invasion of North Africa. Deep in the mountain, in one of the secret command posts carved out of the solid rock, General Dwight D. Eisenhower planned the invasion. The

Today, the duties of the Rock's regiment are mostly ceremonial

ships and troops needed for the invasion assembled in Gibraltar Harbor and in waters close to the peninsula.

During the war, the civilian population of 16,700 was evacuated from the peninsula to French Morocco. When Morocco came under indirect German control, the Gibraltarians were evacuated once again, this time to England and the West Indies. From 1944 to 1951, after the danger had passed, they were gradually returned.

After the war, the Spanish government renewed its demand that Gibraltar be decolonized and returned to Spanish rule. In 1964, Britain considered granting independence to Gibraltar, but the Spanish government objected. In 1965, the United Nations supported Spain's claim to Gibraltar. In 1966, the land frontier between Spain and the colony was closed to all vehicles and trade,

Guards patrol the border;
Spain continues to claim the peninsula

and all Spanish women were prohibited from commuting to Gibraltar—thus causing a serious loss of workers, who were important to the colony's economy. In 1967, in a referendum held by the British government, only 44 of 12,182 Gibraltarians voted against retaining their link with Britain.

When the new constitution of Gibraltar took effect in May of 1969, it contained the statement that Gibraltar is part of the British Crown's dominions and that the Crown's sovereignty over the colony would never be changed against the wishes of Gibraltar's citizens. The Spanish government closed the frontier; 5,000 or so Spanish men could no longer travel to work in the colony each day.

The loss of so many workers disrupted the economy of the colony and the nearby Spanish towns. Gibraltar began importing

Southport Gates show the Rock's rugged stone architecture

workers from Morocco, England, and other countries. The colony also tried to increase its business from tourists. Despite these measures, however, the closing of the frontier caused economic hardship on both sides of the border.

British and Spanish representatives met in Lisbon in 1980 and signed the Lisbon Declaration. Spain agreed to lift border restrictions if Britain would open discussions on the future of the colony. In 1982, the Spanish government opened the border to pedestrian traffic, and in 1984 both governments agreed to act on the Lisbon Declaration by February 15, 1985. Britain repeated its pledge to respect the wishes of Gibraltarians, but agreed for the first time to discuss the question of sovereignty over Gibraltar. At midnight on February 4, 1985, the frontier between Gibraltar and Spain was completely reopened and full trade was resumed.

The People of Gibraltar

Throughout much of Gibraltar's long and turbulent history, its civilian population left the peninsula each time it was conquered. Not until the British conquest of Gibraltar in 1704 did some civilians remain to start the long process of building a permanent population. Starting with the fewer than 100 Spaniards who chose to remain after the British conquest, Gibraltar absorbed a great mixture of immigrants. Sephardic Jews, Spaniards, Genoese, Maltese, French, Portuguese, English, Hindus, Moroccans, and others all found a home on the small peninsula. Out of this mix of ethnic groups and cultures grew a new people, the Gibraltarians.

British customs, like the Changing of the Guard, are preserved

Over the years Gibraltar has become a very close-knit and cohesive community. The sense of unity that Gibraltarians feel has been greatly strengthened by the Spanish closing of the border and by the Spanish demands that Gibraltar be returned to Spain.

Gibraltarians are neither British nor Spanish. They are interested in a great variety of things, from British cricket to Spanish bullfights, from tea and crumpets to *paella* (a spicy Spanish seafood dish), from dancing the Spanish flamenco to the latest dance from England. On the streets of Gibraltar the sound of Spanish music blends with the music of the latest British rock group.

A law enacted in 1900 requires British subjects, unless born on Gibraltar, to obtain residency permits to live there. The law therefore gives official recognition to the idea of a Gibraltarian as distinct from a British subject. A 1962 ordinance established a Reg-

An old etching shows an aqueduct that brought water to the Rock

Gibraltarian wedding customs are similar to those of Great Britain and the United States

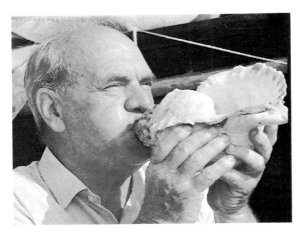

This fisherman uses a shell as a horn

53

ister of Gibraltarians, which contains the names of people born in Gibraltar before June 30, 1925, or their legitimate male descendants, together with a few other persons who have special qualifications. Only these Gibraltarians have the right to live permanently in the colony; all others must obtain residency permits. Now living on the Rock are 19,579 Gibraltarians; 6,676 Britons, mainly military personnel and their families; and 3,532 aliens, mainly migrant workers from Morocco. The workers from Morocco replaced the Spanish workers who were no longer able to enter when the Spanish government closed the border.

All male Gibraltarians are subject to military conscription, and at age 18 every able-bodied male must undergo four months of military training in the Gibraltar Regiment. Thereafter he becomes an active reservist until he reaches age 28 and remains in an inactive military status until he is 41.

A flower seller peddles his colorful wares in Town Square

Our Lady of Sorrows, a Roman Catholic church at Catalan Bay

The church of Santa Maria la Coronada has a Moorish courtyard

The unity that Gibraltarians feel has led to a great tolerance for different cultures, religions, and social customs. Most people in Gibraltar belong to the Roman Catholic Church, and the colony has been the seat of a Catholic bishop since 1910. Gibraltar's Catholic cathedral is named Santa Maria la Coronada. A significant number of Gibraltarians, however, belong to the Anglican Church, and there is also a small Jewish community of Sephardic descent.

Most Gibraltarians are bilingual and speak Spanish and English. Although Spanish is the language commonly spoken in homes, English is used for business, professional, commercial, and governmental purposes. Often the two languages will be mixed together in one sentence, as when a mother tells her child "*Se probibe* to sit *aqui*," or "You're not allowed to sit there." Such blending of languages reflects the unique diversity of Gibraltar.

Yet despite their insistence that they are Gibraltarians, the people of the peninsula also see themselves as members of the British Commonwealth; in that sense they are British. Gibraltarians are not interested in independence, nor do they want to belong to Spain. The overwhelming number of Gibraltarians are

Once a Muslim mosque, Santa Maria is now a Catholic cathedral

Village children pause for a moment of play at Catalan Bay

quite content with their present status as a British colony and see no need for change. Any future determination of the colony's status will have to deal with the strongly stated belief of the Gibraltarians that although they are their own people, they are also intimately and permanently tied to Britain.

Tourists and sailors from many nations mingle with Gibraltarians in the city's busy streets and squares

Ships, Shopkeepers, and Tourists

Most Gibraltarians work either for the Gibraltar government in public administration, in the dockyard as shipbuilders or marine engineers, for the British military base, or in the tourist industry. The British Ministry of Defence owns 51 percent of the land on Gibraltar. Together with the Gibraltar government, the Ministry employs 65 percent of the civilian work force. About 2,000 men, or more than 14 percent of the work force, work in the naval ship-repair yards.

Gibraltar is a free port, where goods may be unloaded, stored, or reshipped without any custom or import duties as long as they are not imported for sale in Gibraltar. There is a large re-export trade in which certain products are brought into the colony for the sole purpose of exporting them again, not for local use.

Fuel for visiting ships is the most important re-export commodity. Since there are no duties on fuel imported specifically for sale to ships, the price of fuel for these ships stays low. Ships are thus encouraged to visit Gibraltar to purchase fuel as well as other provisions. Because Gibraltar is at the gateway to the Mediterranean and possesses excellent port facilities and ship-repair yards,

A tanker in the Strait of Gibraltar waits to load duty-free fuel, an important export item

many ships stop at the colony each year, making a significant contribution to its economy.

Custom duties and income taxes produce most of the colony's revenues. Gibraltar also receives aid from Britain; this aid has been increased since Spain imposed its border restrictions. In

1973, Gibraltar joined the European Economic Community (EEC), also called the Common Market. The organization was formed in 1958 by Belgium, France, West Germany, Italy, Luxembourg, and the Netherlands. In 1973, Denmark, Ireland, and Britain joined the group. The EEC's purpose is to bring about a closer economic

Catalan Bay will become a tourist center

union. Countries who belong to the Common Market try to encourage trade with each other by lowering import and export duties on goods they buy and sell to each other.

Gibraltar has no land available for cultivation. No food is grown on the peninsula; all food must be imported. Gibraltar also lacks any mineral deposits that could be exploited, and must import its oil and fuel. No large-scale manufacturing is possible on the peninsula because of the lack of space, but there is some light industry.

Local manufacturing is limited to small factories, which process tobacco, can fruit and fish, blend coffee, and make clothing. All these products are for re-export and not for local consumption. When the Spanish government closed the border, trade in these goods declined, but with the reopening of the border the colony hopes to re-establish trade. It also plans to expand its markets for these goods to include Morocco and other countries.

In recent years the colony has concentrated on increasing its tourist trade by encouraging large-scale expansion of hotels and beaches. The fishing village of Caleta on Catalan Bay, on the eastern side of the peninsula, is being turned into a tourist resort; new hotels and other facilities are being built. Sandy Bay is also on the eastern side and being developed for tourists.

In addition to expanding the tourist trade, Gibraltar's government officials are encouraging international banks, insurance companies, investment firms, and other companies that offer professional services to open offices on the peninsula. As long as such firms conduct all their business outside the colony, they pay an annual tax of only $500. Some banks, such as the Hong Kong and Shanghai Bank, the Bank of America, and Hambros Bank, have opened offices on the Rock. Government officials hope that many

Both Worlds resort, located on Sandy Bay, is one of the new luxury hotels designed to lure visitors to Gibraltar

Gibraltar's characteristic hill-side houses rise behind the Town Square

Tourists seek bargains on Main Street

others will follow, providing jobs for many Gibraltarians and stimulating the economy with purchases of goods and services from local companies.

On Main Street in the city of Gibraltar are stores that sell goods from all over the world, from sparkling diamonds to cheap plastic souvenirs. Shop windows offer expensive French perfume, Japanese cultured pearls and cameras, Havana cigars, Swiss chocolates, Moroccan bags, African carvings, gold-stitched Indian saris, and amber, jade and gold. There are tartans from the Scottish Highlands, Italian salamis, Turkish water pipes, French cheeses, and countless other products guaranteed to meet any need and satisfy any taste. The whole world is for sale in the stores of Gibraltar.

And the shopkeepers of Gibraltar have learned how to sell to people from all over the world. They are probably the only shopkeepers in the West who have learned Russian, because more Russian ships stop at the port of Gibraltar than at any other port outside the communist world. Gibraltarian shopkeepers say that the Russians spend more freely than other tourists because they do not often have the chance to buy so many different goods.

Food and Water—
Two Problems

Gibraltar must import many of the goods it needs, especially food. At one time, Spain supplied much of the food eaten on the peninsula. As problems with Spain increased, Gibraltar turned to Morocco for fresh fruit, vegetables, eggs, poultry, meat, and other food supplies. Cattle are banned by law in Gibraltar, because there is no land for grazing, so beef is very expensive. But fish is a popular food, with more than 30 varieties for sale in the local fish market on any given day. Four different kinds of lobster, a wide variety of shellfish, and squid and octopus are also available.

Water is a serious problem on Gibraltar, where there are no natural springs or other sources of fresh water. An ingenious sys-

On the arid Rock, water is a precious, expensive commodity

Hardy native plants give the peninsula a tropical air

tem has been designed to catch as much rain water as possible and store it for use during the dry summer months. Thirty-four acres (14 hectares) of the eastern slope of the Rock have been covered with galvanized iron panels, which catch the heavy seasonal rainfall. They direct the water to large reservoirs blasted out of the rock and are capable of holding as much as 16 million gallons. The rain water is later blended with water pumped from wells on the isthmus.

In 1964 and 1968, desalting plants were built to produce fresh water from seawater by removing the salt and then purifying the water. The desalinized water is blended with the collected rain water. If this supply runs short, water is imported from northern Europe—although such imported water is expensive. A separate seawater system provides specially treated seawater for sanitation, fire fighting, and other such needs.

Governor's Street in downtown Gibraltar

The Evolution of Government

Military and not civil law ruled the colony of Gibraltar for more than 200 years, until the end of World War II. The military governor in charge of the colony had complete control over everyone on the peninsula. The absolute rule of the military did not begin to change until 1921, and even then the change was minor.

In 1921, four candidates were elected to a City Council. The majority of Council members, however, were appointed by the military governor, and the work of the Council was strictly limited to certain defined municipal concerns.

Through the years, as Gibraltar grew and prospered, Gibraltarians came to see themselves as distinct from both their Spanish neighbors and their British rulers. They had no desire to become involved in Spanish politics, nor did they wish to become involved in British politics. Gibraltarians increasingly wanted to take more control over their own lives and the affairs of their city-state.

With the end of World War II and the return of all those who had been evacuated, Gibraltarians got involved in local politics. During the war years, some 4,000 civilian men had remained on Gibraltar because they worked in jobs essential to the war effort, mainly in the dockyards. Because Gibraltar was then a military post under wartime conditions, the colony was run like a military barracks instead of a city. Even though they were civilians, the workers were treated like soldiers, and their lack of rights disturbed them. Concern over their status led to the development of the first real democratic government in the colony's history.

The workers formed an organization called the Association for the Advancement of Civil Rights (AACR) to express their concern to military leaders over their lack of rights. After the war was over, the AACR turned its attention to promoting the establishment of representative government in the colony.

The AACR formed an alliance with the Transportation and General Workers' Union (TGWU) to promote the idea of representative government. The joint efforts of these two organizations brought about the creation of a new City Council after the

The Europa Point lighthouse warns ships away from the Rock

war. For the first time, the majority of its members were elected by popular vote.

Today these two organizations no longer work together, and each has gone its own way. The major political party in Gibraltar is called the Gibraltar Labour Party/AACR, which is descended from the original AACR. This organization has faced little serious opposition in recent years.

The constitution adopted in 1964 represented a major step toward self-government. The former City Council was replaced by a new group called the Gibraltar Council, which consisted of the governor (appointed by the British government) and nine other members. The governor alone was responsible for internal security and foreign affairs, and the Council was responsible for general direction and control of the rest of the government.

In the 1967 referendum, Gibraltarians voted overwhelmingly to continue as a colony of Britain. During that year's elections, the association with Britain was a major campaign issue. A new political party was formed, the Integration With Britain Party (IWBP). It won a majority of votes; the AACR Party was defeated for the first time in its history. The British government strongly opposed integrating the colony with Britain, however, so in the next election the IWBP lost and afterward was disbanded.

In 1969, a new constitution established a House of Assembly, with 15 members elected to four-year terms, a speaker appointed by the governor, two ex-officio members, a chief minister, and other government ministers responsible to the House of Assembly. Municipal affairs are handled by one such minister. The military governor, who continues to be appointed by the British government, is the head of the executive branch and is advised by the Gibraltar Council. He appoints the Council of Ministers, which is composed of the chief minister and up to eight other ministers from the party that gains a majority of seats in the Assembly. The governor also remains solely responsible for all internal security and foreign policy matters and has the power of veto over acts passed by the Assembly.

In 1981, Gibraltarians were granted full British citizenship. All Gibraltarians over age 18 and British civilians who have lived for more than six months in Gibraltar are eligible to vote.

The Gibraltar police force is responsible for immigration, residency permits, ambulance service, traffic control, and other police duties. British military forces and the Gibraltar Regiment are responsible for the defense of the peninsula.

Education is free for all children from ages 5 to 15. There are several elementary schools, two secondary schools, some private schools, a technical college for engineering subjects, and a commercial college for women. Scholarships for study at British universities are also available.

Queen Elizabeth's birthday parade

The Barbary Apes

A legend on Gibraltar says that Britain will hold Gibraltar only as long as the Barbary apes continue to live there. The famous Barbary apes, however, are not true apes; they are tailless monkeys, golden-brown macaques who, according to a local story, are descended from the pet monkeys kept by the Moors when they held the Rock. As similar monkeys live on Mount Abyla just across the Strait of Gibraltar in Morocco, there may be some basis for this story.

It is more likely, however, that the apes migrated to the Rock more than 150,000 years ago, when ice covered most of the European continent. During this inhospitable era, they would have found the vegetation high on the Rock suitable for their survival. However the monkeys (or apes, as they are popularly called) got on the Rock of Gibraltar, they are probably the best-known apes in the world.

The apes mature at five years of age and sometimes live to be 20 years old, growing as big as 25 pounds. Although tourists want to see and feed the apes, the apes do not want to see the tourists. They are not particularly friendly and will sometimes attack humans without warning. Still, because they have become the

The famous Barbary apes of Gibraltar are really macaque monkeys

symbol of British dominance, the apes are important to Gibraltarians and to the tourists who come to see them.

In 1910 there were as many as 200 apes on the Rock. But then, for some reason still unknown, they separated into two packs, each of which lived in a different part of the Rock. These two packs engaged in constant warfare, so that by 1913 there were only three female apes left on the entire Rock.

When the government discovered how few apes were left, it started feeding them daily so they would not fight over food. As the apes lived on the upper part of the Rock, and as the Royal Regiment of Artillery was the traditional guardian of this area, the regiment was assigned the duty of feeding the apes every day.

At first the strategy seemed to work, but then the apes went back to their war. By 1924 the government could count only four

74

The apes are considered part of Gibraltar's military garrison; here, a mother and her young

apes on the entire Rock of Gibraltar. Then, for no apparent reason, the fighting stopped and the apes multiplied again. In a few years there were 27 apes. Soon their numbers inexplicably declined once more, this time to only 10 in 1931.

Sir Alexander Godley, the governor of Gibraltar at that time, imported seven apes from Morocco, and the number of apes again increased. Once again, however, the increase was short-lived. By 1939, at the outbreak of World War II, the number of apes was down to 11. And a few years later, in 1943, only seven remained.

At this time Winston Churchill, then Prime Minister of England, heard about the legend of the apes and about their decline. He decided it would be very bad for British morale—and very good for German wartime propaganda—if the apes were to die out. So he ordered more apes brought to Gibraltar.

Seven more apes were imported from Morocco, and this time the newcomers seem to have stabilized the number of apes. Today there are about 40 apes on the Rock, still in two separate packs. A soldier feeds them at government expense each morning and afternoon. The apes are also watched for signs of disease, illness, or injury. Should one of them need medical care, it is taken immediately to the Royal Naval Hospital on Gibraltar and given treatment, or even surgery.

The apes are counted among the numbers of the military garrison on the Rock. Each ape has a name, and all their births and deaths are carefully recorded in the fortress garrison's official records.

Unfortunately, the apes have a habit of stealing anything that strikes their fancy, such as brightly colored or shiny objects. They also have developed the habit of eating automobile windshield wipers and taking things from open car windows. The authorities suggest that tourists not travel by car to see the apes and that all car windows be kept tightly closed when in ape country.

It is easy to see the apes on Gibraltar. One of the packs of monkeys lives in an area of the Rock called Queen's Gate. Tourists can watch the monkeys eat, play, and take care of their families. The best way to view the apes is to stand perfectly still and make no sound that might attract their attention. When they do notice you, the apes will watch you for a while, but if you do not move or make a sound they will ignore you.

The Barbary apes of the Rock of Gibraltar are an important tourist attraction, but like all wild animals, they must be treated

Legend says the fate of the Rock depends on its apes

with some care. Just because they are cared for by the government does not mean that they cannot harm careless tourists.

As long as legend continues to link the Barbary apes to British control of the Rock, the apes will be famous and will be well cared for by the Gibraltarian government.

The Strait of Gibraltar

The Strait of Gibraltar is a narrow passage of water that joins the Mediterranean Sea to the Atlantic Ocean and separates southwestern Europe from northwestern Africa. The channel is approximately 36 miles (58 kilometers) long. At its western extreme, 27 miles (43 kilometers) separate Cape Trafalgar on the northern coast and Cape Spartel on the southern. At its eastern extreme, the strait is just 8 miles (12 kilometers) wide between Point Marroqui in Spain and Point Cires in Morocco. This is less than half the

Tourists look from Europe to Africa across the Strait of Gibraltar

Taken from the Sky-lab space station, this picture shows Spain (top) and Morocco

distance between Dover, England and Calais, France across the Straits of Dover in the English Channel.

The strait averages 1,200 feet (310 meters) in depth; it is deepest in the east and shallowest in the west.

The oceanographic significance of the strait is the way in which it keeps the water of the Mediterranean from becoming salty, like the water of the oceans. The surface water, down to a depth of about 525 feet (160 meters) moves eastward from the Atlantic Ocean into the Mediterranean Sea. Beneath this current is a layer of slower-moving, denser water that contains the ocean's saltiness. This layer also flows eastward, but is turned back into the ocean by the rising seabed of the strait. The surface water flows faster than the heavier, colder, more salt-filled water, so the surface water enters the strait and crowds out the deeper layer.

This two-level movement of water ventilates the Mediterranean. The surface water, filled with oxygen, is favorable to fish life. By shutting out the colder water of the Atlantic Ocean, the surface current also keeps the Mediterranean Sea warm. The Strait of Gibraltar thus prevents the Mediterranean Sea from becoming a shrinking salt lake.

Opposite the Rock of Gibraltar, across the strait, is another large mountain—Mount Abyla, or Jabal Musa, which the Spanish call *Mount Acho*. Together, this 2,782-foot (848 meters) peak and the Rock of Gibraltar were called "the Pillars of Hercules" by the ancient Greeks.

According to legend, the Pillars of Hercules were put in place by the Greek god Hercules, the son of Zeus. Known for his great strength, Hercules was given 12 tremendous tasks to perform. During his labors, he visited the Strait of Gibraltar and planted the two mountains to mark the westernmost point of his travels. To the ancients, the Pillars of Hercules marked the end of the earth. In fact, the Phoenicians encouraged the Greeks to believe that the Pillars were the end of the earth, so that the Greeks would sail no further and the Phoenicians could control all trade beyond the Mediterranean.

From either mountain you can easily see across the strait to the other side. The strait is the only place where you can look from Europe to Africa, or the other way around. Tourists usually climb to high vantage points to enjoy this intercontinental view.

80

Scuba divers prepare for an undersea swim near the Pillars of Hercules; the Mediterranean is kept warm and salt-free by the strait

Horse-drawn carriages (called gharries) tour the peninsula

Gibraltar and Spain: An Uneasy Relationship

Although the British have ruled Gibraltar as their colony for over 250 years, Spain has never formally relinquished its claim to the peninsula. The British claim that the Treaty of Utrecht, which Britain and Spain signed in 1713, gives them possession of Gibraltar and the right to rule it for as long as they want. The Spanish, however, claim that the treaty only temporarily allowed Britain the right to occupy the peninsula. Disagreement has continued for many years, and recently the two countries have had serious disputes over Gibraltar. Fortunately, patient diplomatic negotiations have prevented the trouble from worsening, and progress in settling the dispute seems to have been made.

Article X of the Treaty of Utrecht pertains to Britain's right to rule Gibraltar. Here is that clause:

> X. The Catholic King does hereby, for Himself, His heirs and successors, yield to the Crown of Great Britain the full and entire propriety of the Town and Castle of Gibraltar, together with the port, fortifications and forts thereunto belonging; and He gives up the said propriety, to be held and enjoyed absolutely with all manner of right for

ever, without any exception or impediment whatsoever. But that abuses and frauds may be avoided by importing any kind of goods, the Catholic King wills, and takes it to be understood, that the abovenamed propriety be yielded to Great Britain without any territorial jurisdiction, and without any open communication by land with the country round about.

The Spanish say that this clause supports their claim to rule and govern Gibraltar, while Britain is merely allowed to occupy the peninsula; the British claim that Gibraltar is British—not just a

Travelers from around the world meet on Main Street

British military base on Spanish soil—and that they have the right to possess *and* to rule the peninsula.

The Spanish government took its claim to the United Nations, asking the General Assembly to study all the evidence and render a judgment. In 1965, the United Nations recognized Spain's right to Gibraltar, but the British government did not accept this judgment, and the dispute became more heated as time went on.

On December 16, 1968, the United Nations voted a resolution calling on Britain to end its rule of Gibraltar by October 1, 1969, and to begin negotiations with the government of Spain without delay. Despite this resolution, Britain did not begin discussions with Spain over the question of who should rule Gibraltar.

On May 30, 1969, Britain put forward Gibraltar's new constitution, stating that "Gibraltar is part of Her Majesty's dominions" and that British sovereignty would never be changed against the Gibraltarians' wishes.

The Spanish government, considering this new constitution a step toward granting independence to Gibraltar, closed the border entirely so that no traffic whatsoever could pass between Spain and Gibraltar. A few months later, Spain cut all telephone and cable service with Gibraltar, in order to protest the failure of the British government to observe the United Nations resolution calling for the return of Gibraltar to Spanish rule.

For more than ten years the border remained closed. The end of relations between Spain and Gibraltar caused great hardship, especially for the Spanish workers who had worked on the peninsula. Unemployment in the Spanish towns of La Linea and San

*Gibraltar's troubled
border with Spain*

*Seen from high on the Rock at evening,
Gibraltar's lights fringe the harbor*

86

Roque rose to 20 percent, and the prosperity these towns had once enjoyed ended.

Gibraltar, too, suffered from the border closing. More than 5,000 Spanish workers could no longer come to the peninsula each day to work and had to be replaced. All the food and other goods that Gibraltar imported from Spain had to be imported from other countries. The economic hardships were great on both sides of the border.

Gibraltar slowly adjusted. Food and other products were imported from Morocco and England, and workers came to the peninsula from many countries. Over the years Gibraltar learned to live with its isolation from Spain, and after a while it became prosperous again. But the situation was not good, and no one was happy that the border was closed.

On April 10, 1980, Spain and Britain announced that they had agreed to open the border. Officials from both countries had met in Lisbon and signed the Lisbon Declaration, calling for an easing of border restrictions and for talks aimed at settling the dispute.

The border was not, however, fully opened at once. Spain and Britain disagreed over interpretations of some sections of the document. But at one minute past midnight on December 15, 1982, the border was opened to a limited amount of traffic. Only Spaniards, Gibraltar natives, and British residents were permitted to cross. No tourists could use the border, but at least some progress had been made.

On November 27, 1984, Spain and Britain announced that they had agreed to normalize relations between Spain and Gibraltar, which meant that the free movement of people, goods, and vehicles across the border would be restored; the deadline for normalization was February 15, 1985. An important part of this new agreement was a clause in which Britain agreed to discuss who would rule Gibraltar in the future.

In February of 1985, the border between Spain and Gibraltar was at last fully opened. All people, cars, and trucks could cross, and trade and social relations could begin again after 16 years.

Gibraltarians and their Spanish neighbors could once again move freely across the border. Workers in the Spanish towns of San Roque and La Linea again sought jobs on Gibraltar, and tourists could now visit both Gibraltar and Spain by simply driving across the border.

The first car in 16 years crosses the border in February of 1985

Gibraltar—The Future

Now that normal relations with Spain have been resumed, Gibraltar looks forward to a future of quiet prosperity. Some changes may, however, make that future uncertain.

The British government has announced that, because of economic difficulties in England, it is considering plans to close the naval ship-repair yards at Gibraltar. Such an event would be a serious blow to the economy of Gibraltar. More than 2,000 men—14 percent of the peninsula's total work force—work in these repair yards.

Gibraltarian leaders hope to persuade the British government to keep the repair yards open, or at least to consider selling them to a private shipping company for the service and repair of privately owned ships.

Tourist havens like the Rock Hotel contribute to prosperity

Palm-lined Governor's Parade, in the heart of Gibraltar

In the meantime, tourism has a high priority with officials on Gibraltar. New luxury hotels are being built, such as the Caleta Palace Hotel on Catalan Bay. Popular with tourists, the hotel offers swimming in the warm Mediterranean waters at the foot of the rocks, along with sailing, sunbathing, excellent food, and all the pleasures of a luxury hotel in a tropical climate.

Gibraltar hopes also that instead of stopping for a single day of shopping, tourists from the cruise ships and ocean liners that put into Gibraltar's port will stay for a few days and enjoy more than just the benefits of shopping in a free port. Plans are under way to offer package tours to Gibraltar. Under such plans, a tourist could fly to Gibraltar, enjoy the sun and water of the peninsula for a few days, and then board a cruise ship for a tour of the Mediterranean. After the cruise, the tourist would return to Gibraltar and fly home from there. This way, both the number of tourists and the time they spend on the peninsula would increase.

The future of Gibraltar, both economically and politically, is uncertain. Hard work will be needed to maintain Gibraltar's prosperity and to negotiate a solution to Gibraltar's political problems. Neither can be accomplished quickly. But the people of Gibraltar are enthusiastic, hard-working, cheerful, and hopeful. Their little colony has withstood 15 sieges, many years of warfare, plague, drought, and other disasters. Yet through it all Gibraltar has not only survived but prospered. No one on Gibraltar doubts for a minute that the present troubles will also be overcome and that Gibraltar will continue to be, as it always has been, the key to the Mediterranean.

The **S.S. Camera,** *a cruise ship, anchors below the Rock*

Index

Tariq's Mountain 9
temperature 23
tourism 59, 62–63, 65, 91–92
Transportation and General
    Workers' Union (TGWU) 70
tunnels 20–21, 39

United Nations 48, 85
United States 12
Utrecht, Treaty of 33, 83–85

Versailles, Treaty of 43
Visigoths 30–31

War of the Spanish Succession 32
West Indies 48
Windmill Hill Flats 16
World War I 46
World War II 47–48

yellow fever 44

Zeus 80